DIPPING
INTO
LIFE

40 REFLECTIONS FOR
A FRAGILE FAITH

ALAN HILLIARD
FOREWORD BY TONY BATES

ISBN 9781788123471
Copyright © Alan Hilliard, 2021
All photographs copyright © Alan Hilliard, 2021

Designed by Messenger Publications Design Department
Typeset in Gill Sans, Didot, Rockwell & Dancing Script
Printed by GPS Colour Graphics

Messenger Publications,
37 Leeson Place, Dublin D02 E5V0
www.messenger.ie

ACKNOWLEDGEMENTS

I wish to pay a particular thanks to the team at Messenger Publications for their courtesy, professionalism and encouragement throughout. I'd also like to thank Tony Bates for his forward to this publication and Dr Sandra Cullen for the kind words on the back cover.

Dedication

When I walked up Kilgarron Hill it appeared so steep that I felt my young face was meeting the road. I was three or four years of age and my father walked me to Glaskenny, a townland outside the village of Enniskerry in Co. Wicklow. That was the first of my many visits to that place. As the years passed we had the luxury of a car so Kilgarron Hill was less of problem for me, but I listened to the engine struggle.

The journey to Glaskenny was, for an urban dweller, an afternoon of magic. From a place of brick- and back-lanes we were opened to the wonders of hens and their eggs, sows and their *bainbh* (Irish for piglets) and scenery that never ended. My Aunt May always made us welcome. The Sunday afternoon visits were remarkable with their raucous laughter, generous table and constant adventure. As a child I wanted to hold the sun up in the sky so it'd never set and our day would not come to an end.

This book is dedicated to Aunt May and those who gathered with us, giving us untold chapters of memories and days of delight. It is dedicated to those moments in time that are irreplaceable and are alive in us today. This is especially poignant as many of those who shared those moments are gone ahead of us. The man who held my hand on my first visit there, my father, passed away in December 2019 when I was in the process of writing this book. I also remember in a special way my younger brother Paul, with whom I collected the eggs and fed the sows, and with whom I marvelled at it all on the way back to the brick- and back-lanes of Dublin when the sun had set. The sun set on Paul's earthly life on the 25 October 2020. May they all rest in peace.

Contents

Foreword

My favourite painting in our National Art Gallery is a painting by Diego Velázquez entitled 'The Kitchen Maid with the Supper at Emmaus'. In this painting, a young servant girl in the foreground is leaning over the kitchen sink, listening intently to a conversation taking place in an adjoining room between a stranger and two men who had invited him home for supper. These men had been disciples of Jesus, but in that moment, they don't realise that it is he who is sitting and eating with them. She on the other hand has just realised it's him.

The disciples had met their dinner guest on their journey back to Emmaus in the aftermath of a crucifixion, where the man they'd put their hopes in had been cruelly murdered. His death has been crushing for them because they had believed in him and his vision. They wanted their lives to mean something, but life had taken a turn for the worse and now the future looked bleak. This stranger listened very patiently to their sorrows as they walked together. He gave them space to tell the whole sad story of how their hopes had been dashed.

When it came time to part, they couldn't quite let him go. There was something about this man that they couldn't put their finger on. Something about his voice, his presence, his refusal to be drawn into their despair, his compelling faith that the life they longed for was still possible. They invited him home to extend the pleasure of his company.

I love that it's the simple servant girl who 'gets it' before the two men do. We see her listening and looking like she is holding her breath. We can imagine her thinking to herself, 'Is this the same voice I heard one day in a crowd when that young man spoke to us?' 'What was it about the way he looked at me as I served him food, that made me feel he saw me, that he got me, in a way that no man ever has?' Suddenly, she looks around and recognises him for who he is.

Fr Alan Hilliard for me is like that servant girl. He 'gets it'. He looks at life the way most of us do, but he recognises beauty and mystery where most of us see nothing out of the ordinary. We are more like the two disciples. We may find certain encounters pleasant and the stories we hear entertaining, but that's as far as it goes, most of the time. In those precious moments where we experience the wonder of just being alive, and feel the presence of the divine, we, like that servant girl, suddenly wake up. We 'get it'. We see our lives in a new way. Fear loses its grip.

Alan is also like the curator in an art gallery. In this beautiful book, he has gathered together a series of images and stories that each reveal a truth no less powerful than Velázquez's painting. His *Dipping into Life* recounts conversations that took a turn and revealed some truth that sparkled like a diamond in the rough. A young migrant girl whose story gives us a whole new understanding the Eucharist. Rather than seeing it as some complex theological construct, she explains it as a simple expression of love we carry with us in every moment. Kitchen conversations with people from wildly different corners of the world become windows to the presence of the divine at work in our lives. Adventure stories reveal our hidden strength in times of profound vulnerability. Pages from his own personal journey reveal the author's most life-giving and hard-won insights. Truths we can trust.

Dipping into Life is exactly the book we need for the challenging times we are living through. COVID-19 and its consequences have been traumatic for many and drained the colour out of life for all of us. No matter how much we may believe in prayer, meditation and faith in a loving God, we need help to experience these truths in our everyday lives, particularly when life seems cruel. We need people like Alan to be our guide. So that we, like those two disciples whose hearts have been broken, can have our eyes gently opened and experience the presence of love around us and between us.

Each vignette in *Dipping into Life* is a door we enter to help us see what is extraordinary in the most ordinary and recognise the divine in what is most human.

Tony Bates
Founder of Jigsaw – The National Centre for Youth Mental Health
Professor of Psychology (Adjunct) UCD

Introduction

I spend a lot of my time with people who may not believe what I believe. They may not know the God I know. Church may be far from their lives … and that's okay. It's on me to treat with respect those who believe differently to me and to enjoy their company. There is a goodness in humanity that sometimes takes on a religious frame of reference and at other times takes on another frame of reference. Whatever your view, no one can claim to be better than the other.

A few years ago, I read something written by Timothy Radcliffe. To paraphrase him, he said that going to Church and believing does not make you better than anyone else. Why then do people do those things? His explanation was that you attend Mass, pray, and meet because you believe in a story that is worth keeping alive. This book is a small effort on my part to keep what is an unbelievable story alive. The story of God among us is a story that shines a light on all of life including the moments of sickness, suffering and death. This is not the whole story either – there are moments of joy, wonder, awe, and delight that must be shared.

Thank you for the feedback from my previous two books *Dipping into Lent* and *Dipping into Advent*. A constant word from you was that those books could be applied to the whole of life and not just the seasons they marked and so *Dipping into Life* was conceived.

When I set out writing this book pandemics were the things of movies and novels. Now they are a reality that have made people see the world and their very being differently. Despite the loss of control, people are learning, reflecting, growing, thinking and even praying more. I hope these reflections help you as you reflect, grow, think and pray during crises, difficulties and beyond.

#Absent

'As láithir' – the words used during roll call when I was in primary school that meant someone was absent from class. During the days of COVID-19 we have lived in the presence of a lot of absences. These absences were not punishable offences but necessary measures to keep people safe. They hurt nonetheless, and at times they hurt deeply.

When shopping you couldn't have the usual banter with the shop assistants. They were hidden behind a plastic or glass screen. Even the queue that was growing behind you was the one outside the door. The usual connection and banter was 'as laithir'.

The students at TU Dublin, Bolton St Campus, where I am a chaplain, told me that when they switched off their online classes they felt lonely. They didn't have the usual line up of friends to turn to. The craic and the comradery was 'as laithir'.

Funerals with reduced numbers meant that the support, care, presence, and prayers of those who would gather if they could was most profoundly 'as laithir'.

The absence of these normal 'presences' was painful, even damaging. Regular visitors were even 'as laithir', Grandparents and grandchildren were not present for one another, and thoughts of the presence of loved ones made their absence all the more profound. We were uncomfortable.

The spiritual life is not afraid of absences. It wouldn't want to be because most people who pursue a spiritual path are pursuing something that is missing or absent. The spiritual path seeks understanding, love and meaning. It involves the need to be a part of something or someone.

With so much and so many things 'as laithir' it is often necessary to take time to stare deeply into their absence and, without fear, name them, claim them and never let them be absent again.

The things I thought were so important — because of the effort I put into them — have turned out to be of small value. And the things I never thought about, the things I was never able to either to measure or to expect, were the things that mattered.

Thomas Merton.

· · · · · · · · · ·

#ACoffee

We were sitting over our coffees, talking. Two priests catching up. 'How was the weekend?' I asked, 'Grand', he said. 'What were you up to?' 'Nothing much', he said, 'busy with Mass and people and thinking of what to say and a few laughs'. 'Not boring anyway', I added. 'Certainly not', he said with a cheeky smile. I knew him well enough to know that he had something else to say, but I said nothing. I played at my phone to annoy him even more. A few sips of his coffee and he said, 'Anyway the enemy of life isn't death'. 'What is it?', I asked. 'Boredom', he said. 'No matter how crazy this life is, this one of mine is not boring!' Since that conversation I've made it my business never to be bored.

Once we lose the idea of limits and focus instead on short-term enjoyment, we set in motion long-term disharmonies which have devastating effects on the human situation.

Jonathan Sacks, *Faith in the Future*.

. . . .

#BeingPresent

She was a young girl, a refugee from Bosnia. Her parents were elderly and she did everything for them as their English was practically non-existent. She was always happy and seldom got involved with negativity. She was a great friend to gratitude. I got to know her quite well because I was asked to prepare her for Baptism. Of her own volition, she requested this. While many of her age were nominal Catholics, she was determined to be a committed one.

It was something deep inside her that stirred this request. It wasn't just a matter of feeling left out. My meetings with her were always interesting. I was most anxious before my meeting and conversation with her on the Eucharist, or the Mass as it is more commonly known. She was attending the parish every Sunday so she knew the actions, but I didn't know how much she really understood what was going on. I was further anxious that she'd decide it was way beyond her capacity to understand much less commit to.

When the meeting took place I spoke about occasions when people leave us, that they often leave mementos of their visit. These mementos are objects by which we will always remember them. I told her that Jesus left us this meal and it's not like we just remember him ... this gift is so strong that he becomes present to us. The silence was palpable. I thought to myself, 'That's it, I've lost her now ... and what's more she'll not be back ... ever'.

She spoke, 'When I left my home, I had no time to bring anything with me; we had to get out quickly because the soldiers were coming. There were two things that I had to take so I grabbed them as I left. One was a comb and the other was small mirror. I still have them on the press beside my bed.' She continued, 'The mirror was given to me by my best friend growing up at home. We were everything to one another because I had no brothers or sisters. The comb is the one my grandmother used whenever she combed all the knots out of the long tangles in my hair as she dried it. My grandmother was killed and I don't know where my friend is now. When I was in the refugee camps and feeling very lonely, I didn't want to worry my mam and dad, so I held onto the comb and mirror tightly. In those moments, I'd not just remember my friend and my grandmother but I'd feel them close to me and they'd give me strength.' She paused again and asked, 'is this something like the Mass?' I had no answer and I simply said, 'I think you've got it … lesson over'. I was left wondering who the teacher was!

Christ came to reawaken the human person, and his presence is revealed in the fact that those who acknowledge him relate differently with reality and live intensely in every circumstance that is given to them.

Julián Carrón, *Disarming Beauty.*

#Brendan

According to the 1,200-year-old document *The Voyage of Saint Brendan the Abbot*, St Brendan journeyed across the Atlantic with his crew and was the first European to set foot on the land we now refer to as Canada. Of course when I was a child I was led to believe that this couldn't be true! People scoffed at the idea that it was even possible and suggested the story was complete fantasy! How could anyone get into a boat powered by sail, made of wattle, animal skins and pitch and make it across that large expanse of water? It was too much, even for a Kerryman!

This all changed for me when the explorer Tim Severin set out from Ventry Harbour in 1976. Using the details in *The Voyage of Saint Brendan the Abbot*, he fashioned a boat similar to the one made by the saint, and in May 1976 set off into the Atlantic. In June 1977 word came back that he had made it to Newfoundland. This changed everything. What was previously relegated to the realm of fairy tale and myth became something tangible. Legends

and myths were now more than mere classroom distractions – they held on to truth and possibility. Severin's landing made me ask 'How many more myths and legends have the capacity to make us strive for things beyond ourselves?' Thus began the journey of looking beyond, of holding thoughts in a deeper place, often in silence, and of not taking every dismissive comment or cheap opinion as truth.

There are days when I get distracted or even overcome by vulnerability. I can feel myself bobbing about like Brendan's vessel on an open, turbulent and heaving ocean of uncertainty. This thought may give you particular support – remember that the arrogant hull of the *Titanic* was cracked open by ice mountains and yet the little insignificant wattle boat of Brendan withstood the torment of those seas. Indeed, it was this humble vulnerability that was key to Brendan's successful accomplishment. Severin the explorer discovered this truth. When ice pierced the wattle boat the crew could reach into the water and patch the hole. If the boat was made of wood or steel the vessel would have had no choice but to sink.

'Spiritual but not religious' is like being a fan but not a player.

Murray Milner Jr, *Understanding the Sacred.*

#ChristIsAlive

When I visited Rwanda I met one remarkable priest called Fr Jerome. In size and stature he wasn't unlike the main character from the movie *The Green Mile*. I don't know how he manged to hide himself during the Rwandan genocide, but that is a story in itself that I won't go into now. I remember him telling me about what it was like when he returned to his parish after the genocide. He himself had gone on retreat to Belgium to spend three months praying, just trying to get his head, heart, and soul around all the mayhem of genocide.

When he returned he had nothing save his bible. The Churches were not just closed but they were very often the sites of massacres and still smelt of blood and death. He had no texts, no books. What he said to me then knocked me out. He said, 'Anyway I didn't need them, I realised in the midst of this genocide that I needed to read the word of God alive in my people. I had to find his mercy, his love, his forgiveness, his sacrifices, his Eucharist and his presence in those about me. His word becomes flesh and is written large among them, we as priests have to celebrate this.'

Without resources he had to find a way to bring a divided people together. He selected pieces from the Psalms using them to help people articulate their various feelings of anger, jealously, bitterness, despondency and despair. The group grew in numbers as it was obviously meeting a need among the people. They were poor, they couldn't move and they had no psychologists or counsellors.

A few weeks into the program one of the ladies asked quite innocently if the words they were using were written before or after the genocide. Wow, so real are the emotions of the psalms, which were written over three thousand years before the Rwandan genocide, that they spoke to the lived experience of those who survived it.

Sometimes people take refuge in books alone and forget that God is as present today as he was to those in scripture. People think his word is canonised in sacred text only and forget that his text is about how his word is canonised in his people. This is why I can say that I find myself with an easy challenge. His people are his word made flesh in their love, their capacity to serve, to sacrifice, to give, to laugh and to overcome all forms of adversity with the aid of their own gifts, the support of others and the grace and goodness of God. Finding God in scriptural texts can be quite easy yet quite boring, finding him in human life fills me with hope.

We don't believe instead of doubting;
we believe while doubting.

James K. A. Smith, *How (Not) to be Secular: Reading Charles Taylor.*

. . . .

#Contemplation

Sometimes people don't pray because they feel they're not worthy of it. They think it's not for them. Mention the word 'contemplation' and they just run a mile. They think it's for monks and people who have all sorts of qualifications. Prayer and contemplation are nothing more than simply 'sitting with God'.

This world we live in can be very distracting. Everything gets broken down or torn apart, important concepts are shredded into little bits and pieces. Prayer, and particularly contemplation, allows you to enter into the heart of God knowing that this world beats as one, that there's a harmony in the world. You are more than broken bits and pieces and individual parts. To be at peace you have to see the whole, get the picture of the whole, get the sense of the whole, and it is prayer and contemplation that helps you achieve this.

I find that when I pray in the morning I go out into my day with a greater sense of purpose. I'm not just fiddling with little bits and pieces and trying to fit them all together chaotically.

Perhaps the most important effect of God's love is freedom.

Roger Haight, *The Experience and Language of God's Grace.*

. . . .

#Cousins

Sometimes when I'm out and about I do a bit of 'anger spotting'. There's a lot of it about, and when you've tuned into anger you notice it more – just like the trained plane-spotter, train-spotter or bird watcher, whose trained eye and ear see and hear more than the ordinary passer-by. You notice anger when you are tuned to it. Like when the doors of the LUAS or train open and someone is staring you in the face as you're trying to get off. You're in the way of them getting on ... there's an anger in their eyes, and it's directed at you ... and you've done nothing wrong, you are just trying to get off at your stop.

Anyway, what got me started on this anger thing ... well I was conducting a penance service in a parish. Rather than talk about forgiveness, I talked about the gift of healing, and I gave a little reflection on how much anger there was in the world today. I asked people to reflect on anger in their lives. I can't break the seal of confession but the flood gates opened. It was as if people were given a chance to name something that they kept hidden and that hidden thing was destroying them.

Don't get me wrong. Not all anger is bad, sometimes anger is justified. In the face of wrong-doing righteous anger can have a place, but it can't last for ever. It is given to you to to alert you to something that has to be faced up to and acted upon. Righteous anger has some very nasty first cousins. They are plain old anger, jealous anger, vindictive anger or self-righteous anger. Put these guys together in the one room and there is some family battle. If your anger isn't righteous but is one of these nasty first cousins well then, let go of it as it will only drag you down.

A mild answer turns back wrath,
but a harsh word stirs up anger.

Proverbs 15:1

#Distracted

In the 1990s I was in an obscure part of Australia. I misread my bus timetable and, without any smartphone to correct me, missed my bus. I had two hours to wait and to my delight I spied a bookshop. It was 'eclectic' to borrow an overused term. Within minutes I had an armful of books, I paid for them and my appetite for caffeine, sugar and knowledge was greatly stimulated. The one book that I got stuck into was penned by a Canadian sociologist. My one regret today is I can't put my hand to this book; it's either on loan or at the bottom of a box somewhere. His writing had a very clear and uncomplicated style – always I think the sign of real intelligence. One line, about the coming twenty-first century, stayed with me for years and years. Sometimes I feel the Holy Spirit puts these lines in my spiritual pocket so they can be pulled out when needed. I have a number of phrases like this. The line in this book went something like this: 'beware the gatekeepers'.

I didn't fully understand its significance until much later. When I look at the rise of social media and see what has happened with Cambridge Analytica I hear those words 'beware the gatekeepers' echo around my mind and soul. There are millions of gates now, which gatekeeper do I look to?

Maybe for too long there were only a few solitary gatekeepers. They told people what the truth was and there was no choice but to believe them. Like the rather authoritarian parish priest who had it in for his new young curate. He said to a parishioner 'when you come to my Mass you hear not only what Jesus said but what he meant to say!'

Every day 11 billion notifications are sent to more than 1 billion users of Android apps ... all trying to open gates to get you into their field. The 11 billion are distractions from study and conversations with people who matter. They are 11 billion opportunities to be distracted from meditation and prayer, even 11 billion distractions so we can be distracted from earlier distractions!

I've noticed that my mind is finding it hard to settle and as I'm concentrating on one thing I find my mind is jumping to another. I was frightened recently when I read a line from the philosopher Matthew Crawford who said, 'Distractibility might be regarded as the mental equivalent of obesity'.

Jesus never uttered a word of propaganda. He merely answered the thirst of those two (Andrew and John) with an invitation, so that they themselves could draw their own conclusions.

Julián Carrón, *Disarming Beauty*.

· · · · · · · · ·

#Enchantment

The one thing that I dislike about secularism is that it asks me to seek meaning and life in the secular world alone. I am asked to believe that 'society' itself has become the source of everything. Yet, more and more societies are falling apart as they face ever greater moral challenges. Secularism brings with it a growing interest in political and national identities as people try to chart new ways of belonging and new sources for the foundations of civil society without religion. Those who have a religious belief have to speak the language of sociology more and more just to be 'relevant'. Once your language changes you lose your power – in actual fact you give it away, particularly if it is the language of conviction.

The language of secularism is often associated with Nietzsche telling us that 'God is Dead'. However, in 1881 he wrote a note saying, 'the political madness at which I smile just as my contemporaries smile at the religious madness of earlier times, is above all secularisation, the belief in the world and the rejection of a world "beyond" and "behind"'. Even the one who contributed to the evolution of secularism can see its limitations and its fanciful errors!

Whether you are deeply religious or secular there is room for wonder. I love the line from Patrick's Kavanagh's poem 'Raglan Road' where he invites you to walk along 'the enchanted way'. Maybe the nature of religious expression is changing – it might be moving away from its largely institutional identity into something more personal. Belief may have a greater element of choice rather than the heavy-handed impositions of the past. Enchantment invites people to acknowledge that science and religion are not opposing forces but are common hosts on the path towards enchantment.

Wherever you go you need to have language and methodologies that lead to the world of enchantment. One thing learned from the past is that 'enchantment' cannot be created by a school timetable. Just like a religious sensibility you cannot switch it on and off to suit absent policy makers. It is a stirring of the soul and it has its own timetable. Luckily the world does not have to be 're-enchanted'. You only have to cultivate reverence and recognition for what is already present.

There must be more to life than science. The 'more' is an inner garden of the imagination that each of us should be allowed to cultivate, where we should be encouraged to dwell for at least some part of our days and lives.'

Mark Patrick, Hederman, *Living the Mystery.*

. . . .

#Eucharist

The Polish writer Sławomir Mrożek observed, 'Once upon a time, we blamed our unhappiness on the management of the day – God. We concurred that he ran the business badly. We sacked him and appointed ourselves managers'. He follows up on this concept with the idea that the modern person is surrounded by others at the equivalent of a fancy-dress stall, where they can change their image endlessly so that they are disbarred from finding their true selves, for if they do then the party is over! As another writer says – we've gone from keeping up with the Joneses to keeping up with the celebrities!

So much of what goes on in the world today is in opposition to the basic precepts of Christian faith and indeed many other faiths. The New Testament refers to the Church as the Body of Christ – everything about Christianity is 'we'. For people like St Oscar Romero being the Body of Christ was more than just an issue of community. For him it was to feel the pain of his people, even those who were caught up in its dark side. His final words were 'may God have mercy on my assassins'. He was all too aware that the essential goodness of a person can be obscured by the prevailing ethos of their time. The Eucharist is far from a fancy-dress shop – even though people do dress up going to Mass. When you sit with love your real self is exposed. If you find something in yourself that you are not happy with, you can ask for God's abundant mercy and forgiveness. When you find the many things for which you can be grateful you can offer thanks too. For those bits of life that are burdensome you can ask others to share your load.

The Eucharist is such a wonderful gift. It is sometimes, however,

obscured by 'the management'. As a colleague said to me once, 'I never tire of the mystery of the Eucharist though I can often get browned off with the way it is celebrated'.

Even religion has degenerated, in some quarters, into a cult of feelings and pious emotions and, at best, a vague sense of fellowship and kindness and general optimism about one's neighbour.

Patrick F. O'Connell, *Thomas Merton, Early Essays, 1947–1952*

#Exile

There was a period in history when the people of Israel were in exile. They were taken from Jerusalem to Babylon for forty-eight years. Their homeland was far away, and they wondered if they'd ever return. It was a historical event, but it has become a powerful narrative of survival.

What the scholars say about exile might help people deal with some of the fall-out from this difficult time. It is possible, during times like these, to feel a sense of being lost or of being like strangers in your own home. For those who experienced exile there were three main threads of thought present. Firstly, people said that exile was a well-deserved punishment; secondly, they said it was the same as death and thirdly, they focused on creating a stunningly refreshing idea of the future.

It is easy to slip into the first or second threads, as they can be the default positions in crisis. It is easy to slip into shame-based thinking, saying that this difficulty is deserved because I've got too complacent, or I can feel that because there is so much I can't do, I am experiencing a living death. The third option is the one that is the most life giving, as those who historically lived through exile attest. This option is to sing against the pressures and difficulties of present reality and to dance towards a future that isn't clear yet. Don't be overcome by the theory that your hardships are punishment or death, make it about a future as yet not revealed.

There were many who spent time in exile during the world wars whose writings give encouragement and hope. One among them is the great theologian of hope, Jürgen Moltmann. He studied science and maths until 1944, when he was drafted into the German Army. He surrendered to the first British soldier he met and spent his years between 1945–48 as a prisoner of war in Belgium, Northern England, and then finally Scotland.

Totally without hope one cannot live. To live without hope is to cease to live. Hell is hopelessness. It is no accident that above the entrance to Dante's hell is the inscription: 'Leave behind all hope, you who enter here'.

Jürgen Moltmann, **Theology of Hope**

31

#Freedom

Dachau was closer to the City of Munich than I realised. For some reason I thought it'd be lost in the countryside – out of sight and out of mind. On the tour I discovered that it was built in the early 1930s. It was built to incarcerate not any particular ethnic group but anyone who disagreed publicly with Hitler's policies. This changed with time.

The tour was both sombre and intriguing. There was a lot to remember, but there was one part of the tour I'll never forget. At the end of the tour the guide described the days when the German soldiers left the camp, leaving the prisoners in their billets. Once the prisoners became aware that the soldiers were gone they wanted to leave the camp, but the Allied officers in charge of the prisoners insisted that they stayed where they were. Days later the Allied troops found their way into the camp and liberated those prisoners. The troops were shocked at what they found.

The Allied camp commanders were right. If the prisoners made their way onto open roads they may have died or they may also have been attacked by the advancing troops, who would not have known from a distance who the approaching people were.

I stood in silence for a while as the tour was ending. A still small voice made its way into my soul and said 'it is often more difficult to manage freedom than captivity'. This still small voice and the image of that prison camp has come back to me on many occasions when I faced changes with their accompanying fresh challenges and opportunities.

As it was expressed by W.B. Yeats, and none have said it better, 'too long a sacrifice can make a stone of the heart.'

John Hume, *Personal Views, Politics, Peace and Reconciliation in Ireland.*

#God

I believe in God. I believe in a force that holds me in cupped hands especially when things are against me. The world can be my enemy and God's at the same time.

The first thing that ever existed according to our Bible was not darkness or light, it was chaos and it was God who tamed it. This work continues today as it did in the beginning and yes indeed, sometimes it appears to be futile – chaos may appear to reign supreme. But in the still silence of God there is always an order. There has to be as love brings with it an order that rises above chaos. Love can be present strongly among people in the most tumbled-down house and love can be present in the most tumbled-down world. It holds things together even if there is a real fear that everything could fall apart in one swift moment.

The great evidence of that love for me is the gift of joy. I do not mean raucous laughter or false happiness. I mean the joy of knowing, believing, and feeling that all is well. There is a joy that comes as gift when love touches us – joy is the scent of that love and it can linger long, and we can linger long in those cupped hands.

Love, in fact, is the vocation which includes all others; it's a universe of its own, comprising all time and space – it's eternal.

From the Autobiography of St Teresa of the Child Jesus
In the Office of Readings, 1st October.

. . . .

#Gratitude

Emotions play a very important part in people's lives. They guide, shape and often determine how people respond to situations. Emotions too can linger. Feelings of joy can tell you that all is right with the world whereas feelings of despair and those feelings associated with depression can burn a painful hole into your heart, leaving you quite despondent.

I was watching a series on television recently. The main character was a barrister. He was a complex character. While good at his job, his personal life was in tatters. He was also quite humorous and entertaining. One day, while in conversation with his assistant and reflecting on the outcomes of a case, he came out with a nugget of wisdom that bowled me over. He said 'gratitude is often the shortest-lived emotion'!

All too often people hang on to the wrong emotions. Wrong in that they could choose to let them go but instead choose not to. Emotions of resentment, bitterness, despair linger far too long in us. People forget that emotions are often teachers trying to tell them something. They hang on to the emotions and so remain stuck.

Every night I try to think of three things in the day that has passed that I can give thanks for. Sometimes it requires a bit of a struggle because something may have happened in that day that has obscured any sense of gratitude. However, and to be honest, there are always at least three things to give gratitude for. The little bit of wisdom that 'gratitude is often the shortest-lived emotion' has forced me to dwell on those things I give thanks for. When I think of the things in my day that I can say 'thank you' for, rather than swallow them quickly I savour them and dwell on them. I have often given this bit of advice to people who are struggling with a spot of depression, and they've come back to me to say 'thank you'.

Dorothy Day believed that a Church made up of spiritually dedicated and socially committed people was the antidote for a corrupt capitalist system. 'We have all known the long loneliness and we have learned that the only solution is love and that love comes from community.'

Daniel J Groody, *Globalisation, Spirituality and Justice.*

. . . .

#Hope

Whenever my faith needs a boost or a sorting out there are a number of people I spend time with. One is a student by the name of Peter. He is married with three lovely children. I got a text from him a few weeks ago, 'Guess what Fr Alan, I got a house. I was very blessed because in two days I and my family were going to be homeless'. He finished with, 'God is good'. I phoned him this week to find out how he is getting on in his new home in Dublin. 'We have nothing, I've just got carpet but we can get nothing because everything is closed because of COVID-19, but God is good', he said. I called him to chat to him about the COVID-19 pandemic. I like his take on things and he simply said 'This too will pass, one day it will be over'.

The Risen Lord is among us to tell us to hope. He encourages us to hope now and to hope beyond the grave. The whole story of scripture is a story of God trying to restore hope among his people by giving them leaders like Moses, prophets like Ezekiel, great women in scripture like Ruth, but eventually, to nail the message home, he sent his Son. He is one who walks among people. He doesn't lord it over people but serves them. He starts with people where they are. If people are lost in despair or raucous with joy he starts there. If you doubt this please note that he didn't lose the head when he met those who betrayed him. He simply said, 'peace be with you', and in the post-Resurrection narratives he shared breakfast rather than suppers. A subtle message – start your day well, and start it in peace, and all will be well.

Tonight we acquire a fundamental right that can never be taken away from us: the right to hope.

Pope Francis, Easter Vigil 2020.

. . . .

#Leaders

I'm sure Noah would never get his ark completed today. The flood would well and truly have passed over him before he started building. There are so many rules and regulations governing the simplest of tasks. There are mountains of paper work that have to be completed, forms to be filled, permissions to be got and standards to be reached.

He'd have to complete an environmental impact statement, let the planning authority know that he was creating a temporary structure, undergo a health and safety audit, let the tax office know where he got the money from just in case he was laundering and finally he'd have to ensure that all the animal rights organisations were happy with the accommodation he was hoping to provide to the animals.

The world has become a very complicated place. Some of us may dream of an idyllic, simple life where things can be done with ease and basic comradery, but that dream is getting further and further from view. It's as if the world has been made to destroy initiative and keep the status quo in place. On reflection this is not new. I'm sure Noah had equivalent problems in his day. Sure, Jesus was a leader too, and it was the status quo who had him crucified.

Managers are people who do things right, leaders are those who do the right thing.

Charles Handy, *Understanding Organisations.*

. . . .

#LivingAndBelieving

I recently read a book about well-being. The author was looking at what was going on in the world and why people were so depressed – why there were so many incidents of mental illness. He had first-hand experience of both. Many of the scenarios he presented I found to be inspiring, especially because they involved the insights of ordinary people. Reading this book, I became convinced that most of the problems people face come from the fact that they are disconnected from the ideas that can make a difference and, in particular, from creation.

One of the scenarios in the book concerned Native Americans. Those living on reservations experienced high rates of suicide and mental illness. These rates were unsurprisingly highest in those reservations where people had no power over their lives. Their food was cooked for them and their lives were time-tabled. The communities with the greatest control over their lives had the lowest suicide rate and those with the least control had the highest rate. Whatever about these outcomes there is one line that rang true for me. An elder of the Crow Tribe was interviewed in 1890 by an anthropologist, and he was asked about the tragedies that had befallen his people and the way they were asked to live in the reservation. He simply said, 'we are being asked to live a life we don't understand'. How many of us could say the same?

Two hermits lived together for many years without a quarrel. One said to the other, 'Let's have a quarrel with each other, as other men do'. The other answered, 'I don't know how a quarrel happens'. The first said, 'Look here, I put a brick between us, and I say, "That's mine". Then you say, "No, it's mine". That is how you begin a quarrel'. So they put a brick between them and one of them said, 'That's mine'. The other said, 'No, it's mine'. He answered, 'Yes, it's yours. Take it away'. They were unable to argue with each other.

Rowan Williams, **Where God Happens – Discovering God in One Another.**

#Mangolia

There is the story of a lady in Dublin who was having constant problems with damp stains on a wall in one her bedrooms. The black marks got worse and worse no matter how much she cleaned them. Eventually she called on the services of a local painter who came in to assess the situation. He wanted the job but didn't want to appear too enthusiastic. He knocked on the wall a few times, took out a measuring tape, scrapped off some of the stained plaster, sniffed it, and studied it while his glasses remained perched at the end of his nose. He stood back, hands on hips, interrupted only by an odd and infrequent rubbing of his chin and squirming of his face, and eventually he said, 'Well Missus, you'll be glad to know that it's nothing that a few litres of mangolia [this is not a misspelling] won't sort out'.

I learned the hard way not to focus on problems. I learned the hard way to look deeper to see what is causing them. Sometimes you'd love the equivalent of a few litres of 'mangolia' to put a coating on the problems to get rid of them, but they don't go away. You could be distressed because you are hurt, ignored or let down. You can be upset because you are being spoken about in ways that aren't true or are true but in speaking of them someone has broken your trust. If you don't dig deep to find the underlying problem, you will end up going around in destructive circles.

When God got upset with the people he rescued from Egypt he referred to them as a 'stiff-necked people'. He got upset because they lost their gratitude and substituted it with greed. If God can't avoid getting upset ... there's not much chance for you or I!

Think of when Jesus got upset in the temple with the traders.

I think it was less about what they were doing and more about what they were neglecting. There is a sacred space in each person that is often allowed to get cluttered or distracted. It's hard for those who love you not to get upset when they believe that there are better things for you. Take an opportunity to declutter … start with any upset that is taking up valuable space and using up unnecessary energy. You can give your mangolia to somebody else whose is happy enough to paper over the cracks.

You can wear all the protective gear you like,
but you cannot protect your soul.

Pietro Bartolo and Lidia Tilotta *Lampedusa, Gateway to Europe*.

· · · · · · · ·

#Mary

She was an elderly lady. She had lived a very full life and a very happy one, but now it was time to move on. Diagnosed with a disease that would bring her earthly life to an end in a few months, she enjoyed Mass and really delving into things spiritual. She wasn't a naïve Catholic by any means. Arguments (justifiable) with her local parish meant she shied away from attendance in that place, which made it more difficult for her to get to Church, but she had a deep prayer life and a well-integrated spirituality.

She wanted to see me so I called by. Eventually we got to what was troubling her. 'I just can't pray any more. I do my best but I just get distracted and seem to be going nowhere.' I said that I wasn't surprised with the amount of medication she was on. I told her it'd be hard to focus on anything. I could see her disappointment as not only did she want to pray, she needed to pray.

I asked her did she know the Hail Mary? She looked at me puzzled. 'Of course I know the Hail Mary'. I think my question infuriated her. 'Do you know that line "Pray for us sinner, now and at the hour of our death. Amen?"' 'I do', she replied. I explained to her that when I can't pray I bring that line to mind. 'Why?' she asked. 'Well', I said, 'it reminds me that Mary is always praying for me, especially when I can't pray. So, I just join in with her as she prays with me'. I continued, 'I just sit there thinking of her praying for me'.

A tear came to her eye. 'Thank you so much, I've prayed that prayer so many times and I never thought about that line in that way.' We sat for a while and chatted and then she said, 'It's time for my afternoon nap, I'm off to lie down. When my head goes on the pillow I will think of Mary praying for me and I'll join her'.

If Christ and Jesus are the archetypes of what God is doing, Mary is the archetype of how to receive what God is doing and hand it on to others.

Richard Rohr, *The Universal Christ*.

#Mathematician

Blaise Pascal was a seventeenth-century mathematician and scientist, and he hadn't the easiest of lives. His mother died when he was three, his father died later in life and, before his father died, he was inspired by the care given by two doctors who had great religious faith. He had what you could call an intellectual conversion to the ways of the Almighty. But later in his life he had some amazing insight into God! This insight was way beyond a mere intellectual conversation and his life was never the same again.

The words he wrote that captured that moment were quite extraordinary in that they lacked any rational purpose – they were very scattered – but he tried to capture something of the nature of God. I thought that as a mathematician his words would have been perfectly organised and balanced! And what did he do with that bit of paper that he wrote on? He sewed it onto the inside of his coat. When he wanted to be reminded of his encounter with God he would just open his coat and read the words he wrote. These words were only discovered when he died.

Here are a few lines from those words, sewn inside his coat:

Forgetfulness of the world and of everything, except GOD.
He is only found by the ways taught in the Gospel.
Grandeur of the human soul.
Righteous Father, the world has not known you, but I have known you.

#MentalHealth

It is not uncommon for a student to sit in front of me whose opening words are 'me head is melted'. Students tend to let things build up until a crisis or a deadline comes along and everything falls apart. I deal a lot with students who are involved in subjects relating to building and the environment. When they'd settled down, I would often ask them, 'What's stress?' They'd inevitably say, 'When your head is wrecked . . .like mine is now!'

I would push them a bit and say, 'Well you are an engineer … what's stress?' They'd give the same answer, and I'd push a bit harder and say, 'What's the definition of stress from an engineer's point of view?' Eventually they'd come up with the answer: 'Tension over area'. I'd continue, 'If I built a bridge with ten arches and all the tension was resting on one of those arches what'd happen?' 'The bridge would collapse', they'd say. 'Okay then … think of yourself as that bridge … where is all your tension resting at present?' With a bit of encouragement they'd realise that they were putting too much pressure on their brain and ignoring other supports in their life.

If you put too much pressure on any one part of your life, there is a risk of collapse. If you put too much pressure on any one part of your being, there is a risk of collapse too. The body, soul, mind and emotions are given to you to spread the load. The same is true of your family and friends, and of support services and those things that help you to discover your beliefs and values. When you are in good form, you are aware of all these 'arches' in your life. The load is spread quite evenly. When you are in bad form, you put too much pressure on one 'arch', that single arch just can't carry the load!

Depression and anxiety might, in one way, be the sanest reaction you have. It's a signal saying — you shouldn't have to live this way, and if you aren't helped to find a better path, you'll be missing out on so much that is best about being human.

Johann Hari, *Lost Connections*.

· · · · · · · · · ·

#MoneyInYourPockets

I felt a right fool. I cycled to the shops to get a few bits of shopping. When I got to the cash register, I fumbled about but couldn't find my money. I left the groceries with the assistant, cycled home for my wallet, went back to the shop, paid for the items and headed home, getting caught in the most horrendous shower. I was soaked through. I peeled the clothes off my body to get into a warm shower and in the process cleared my pockets of wet tissues and other items that absorbed the rain. You can only begin to imagine how I felt when I reached into my back pocket to find the (wet) fifty euro note I had put there prior to my shopping expedition. I had gone up to the register, cycled home, cycled back to the shop, cycled home again in the rain and apart from the initial expedition all totally unnecessary – especially the bit in the rain!

There are occasions when I go round like a fool, feeling that there is nothing left in the tank. I am psychologically and emotionally drained. There is always a bit in reserve but for many reasons I, like many others, don't believe it. There are parts of you that don't get used up. Resources you don't believe you have and so you fall and don't get up. There are moments of delight when you share a journey with someone and they discover a gift in you that you never knew you had. Their insight makes you marvel at your own being. This is especially joyous when the gift names something that you've been looking for. Dig deep; believe in yourself. Don't let yourself feel like a fool for too long!

I find a star-lovely art in a dark sod.

Patrick Kavanagh.

#MrUnflappable

I'm always amazed at how some people can get the better of situations and never seem perturbed or angry – at least not on the surface. I often wonder if they go home and throw a tantrum when no one is watching!

I've met many people who just seem to be able to take life in their stride. They have developed a disposition whereby nothing seems to bother them. I'll never forget one man. He was a highly qualified psychotherapist and he exuded coolness. You could tell that nothing ruffled him. His hair was perfectly combed, his clothing was perfectly coordinated and nothing was ever out of place.

One of his colleagues confirmed my observations saying he was unflappable. He went on to tell me a story. One evening Mr Unflappable was going home to dinner and he had my friend in the car with him. When he pulled up into his driveway there was another car already parked there. As they walked by this car you could not help but notice that the entire passenger side was in shreds having obviously suffered a collision of a most serious kind.

He stopped and looked the car up and down. The visitor was expecting a tirade of frustration and he simply said, without raising his voice, 'Oh dear, my wife seems to have crashed the car again'. To which the visitor replied, 'What do you mean again … there's thousands of pounds worth of damage done … and that's all you are going to say … oh dear!!!' Mr Unflappable looked at his visitor, smiled and said, 'Life is too short for anger and blame'.

And so it is … you can spend your life being angry. Every precious moment of your life can be consumed by anger and it doesn't change anything … it definitely won't fix the car. Don't shorten your life today by getting lost in anger and blame … savour the sweetness of life, don't poison it.

Sancho Panza divides the world into those, like himself, who were born to sleep and those, like his master, who were born to watch.

Jonathan Crary, *24/7.*

· · · · · · · · ·

#OnYerBike

I was cycling up Sandford Road in the direction of Milltown, and I pulled up at the traffic lights at the junction of Merton Drive. I shared the space with a few other cyclists. A car was pulling across the road from Merton Drive and was let into the space by a kindly motorist. When he pulled into the queue of traffic his bumper was ever so slightly in the cycling lane. Not a problem … no one wanted his tail end sticking out into on-coming traffic on the other side of the road. There was a courteous facilitation of his plight.

A fellow cyclist appeared out of nowhere. He stopped and uttered some very colourful expletives to the motorist. The other cyclists and I looked at one another, wondering what his problem was and then watched with amazement at what happened next. Having finished his tirade he belted off towards Milltown, breaking two red lights within a hundred yards of each other. This reflection is not about the merits of cycling; it is more about anger. There is a lot of it about. You don't have to be long on the road whether you are on a bike, in a car or some other vehicle to spot anger, even to feel it. I suppose people get angry because they feel someone is in their way or that another person has done something foolish. Sometimes, people do get in the way. Sometimes, people are foolish. An angry response, however, helps no one. As a matter of fact anger begets anger. It doesn't go away and it can leave you feeling sorry for yourself or even feeling a little self-righteous. I'm right and the whole world is wrong!

The Book of Sirach tells us that,

> **Unrighteous anger cannot be justified,**
> **for a person's anger tips the scale to their ruin.**

Anger can be justified if, for instance, it alerts you to wrong-doing, but you have to turn your attention to what is wrong, fix it and then lose the anger. If you hold on to it … it can become very toxic.

The worship of the one God liberates human beings from all possible idols and earthly powers. Thus their freedom depends on this capacity for transcendence.

Jürgen Habermas et al, *An Awareness of What is Missing*.

#Play

During 2020 many people have been introduced to the concept of 'working from home', which made it more difficult to know when work ended and play began. But I suppose you really have to realise that work ... the purpose of work ... is to give people time to relax, and the whole thing about creation is that it doesn't depend on work alone. Creation is not put in place to keep you busy all the time, but rather it is there so you can sit back and enjoy its beauty.

A friend of mine said to me many years ago, 'You know Alan, organise your play and the work fits into place'. It was a great line, and it has helped me more often than not to put my mind to organising places and times to relax rather than just being consumed by what's going on in the world.

The people of the Old Testament invented Sabbath, this was an attempt to institutionalise rest and play. I know we associate Sabbath with a day of rest or a day of worship, and many people do worship, and that's a very important part of their lives, but Sabbath was invented by people who wished to remind themselves that they weren't slaves anymore.

Yahweh is a Sabbath keeping God, which fact ensures that restfulness and not restlessness is at the centre of life.

Walter Brueggemann,
Sabbath as Resistance, Saying No to the Culture of Now.

· · · · · · · · · ·

#PostModernism

Ireland, like many countries, fought long and hard to have a modernist state that would become a strong entity holding the people together. The nation managed its own post offices, churches, governmental bodies and other centralised structures that helped the nation progress. There was no room for manoeuvre – you followed the dictates of central authority that claimed to know best and which acted in your best interest, or so people were led to believe.

Post-modernists believe this way of living is now past. Modernity was seen as a long march towards order, but there were more and more occasions emerging when the price of holding order in place was too much and could not be paid. Indeed, it was a price that could not be paid because the price was human life on

a vast scale. And so people have attempted to move beyond this order by replacing it with a seeming chaos. Centrality has been replaced with individuality. What was once a life that was stable, known, defined and reliable is no more. People have moved beyond a world of community and togetherness and toward a world of individuals and their freedom.

These changes may be lauded by some and lamented by others, but the important thing to ask is whether these shifts have made you happier or better off. Reinhart Koselleck offers a description of the world of today in which it is akin to trying to climb a steep slope in order to reach a peak. The slope is too steep to stop and camp, no construction would survive the crosswinds and rainstorms, so you have to keep climbing. What is on the other side, you cannot know until you reach the peak.

Jesus lived between competing worldviews. He lived between Galilee and Jerusalem, between the local synagogue and the temple. He crossed borders to show the love of the Father, as in the case of the Good Samaritan and the Syrophoenician woman. At the end he was stuck between the worldview of the High Priest and that of Pilate. His death and resurrection told us, unlike many other ideologies, not to be afraid of what lies on the other side.

The self-styled liberators from poverty are too often those who want to preach, rather than listen, to the poor.

Paul Farmer and Gustavo Gutiérrez in *Conversation, In the Company of the Poor.*

#PrayerInSydney

Over two hundred years ago, on the 3 May 1820, two Irish priests arrived in Sydney. One was a Cork man, John Joseph Therry, and the other a Monaghan man, Philip Connolly. Connolly was the senior and a good friend to officialdom. He ended up in Hobart where he built the first Catholic Church in the Antipodes described as 'a rude, barn-like room, unceiled, unplastered, and floored with loose boards that creaked and moved with every step'.

Connolly was overshadowed by Therry whose four-year appointment ended up as forty-four years in the colony. He didn't build ramshackle buildings. One of his first churches was none other than St Mary's Cathedral in Sydney. The foundation stone was laid by governor Macquarie in 1821 and the first Mass was eventually celebrated there twelve years later in December 1833. Throughout the project, doubt was raised as to whether there'd be enough Catholics to fill St Mary's.

In a tough and prejudiced environment, Therry was known

and loved for his dedication to duty. He was pulled across rivers by rope to hear the confessions of people who were dying. He always kept one spare horse saddled so that when he returned from one mission he could head out immediately to another one.

While he was initially paid by the government of the day, he lost his salary because he upset the Anglican clergy following a typing error in the *Sydney Gazette*. He survived without a salary as his people were willing to support him. The harsh treatment he received from the government made him even more popular among his people.

Therry didn't step into a vacuum though. The earliest priests were convicts, one of whom was James Dixon, who in 1800 was granted permission to exercise his priestly duty. This ended following the Castle Hill rebellion in 1804. The authorities viewed Dixon's liturgical gatherings as a cover for seditious meetings that led to these riots. His right to minister was suspended.

Between 1804 and 1820 what happened to the Catholic community in Sydney? Some priests came and went but people simply prayed. In one house in Kent St, which runs down the centre of Sydney today, people kept the Blessed Sacrament that a priest left behind before he was deported back to Ireland. Catholic piety thrives in the absence of ecclesial structures.

Attention isn't just about what you're doing right now. It's about the way you navigate your whole life: it's about who you are, who you want to be, and the way you define and pursue those things.

James Williams, *Stand Out of Our Light*.

. . . .

#Rooms

In this reflection I want you to use your imagination. I want you to picture a four-roomed house. The first room is represented by the letter 'P'. This is the physical room. This is where you exercise and take care of yourself. You know what happens if you neglect your exercise. The next room is the 'M' room. The 'mental' room where you read, play games, even back a few horses, or do crosswords just to expand the plasticity of the brain. The third room is the 'E' room. The room of emotions where you know you are loved and where you too love! The last and final room is the 'S' room. This is the room of spirituality and meaning. It is characterised by a spirituality that gives your life a context.

The power of this image lies in how you understand it. Most problems occur because you overspend time in one room and neglect the others. Sometimes this is through no fault of your own. Think of people who spend long hours trying to stay physically strong. They can become emotionally, mentally and spiritually exhausted. Think of the student who spends hours studying to the neglect of everything else, or of the person who has experienced the breakdown of a relationship or a bereavement, and who has become a prisoner of the emotional room.

COVID-19 brought a lot of this imbalance into people's lives. Whether it is the physical, mental, emotional or spiritual rooms that COVID-19 has kept you from, the balance is hard to restore. It's like when you have a room in your house that you don't go into – it's a mess and you don't want to be reminded of how bad things are in there, so you stay away.

I firmly believe that most of the problems of today's world exist because people don't go into the spiritual room or the confuse the emotional room with the spiritual. The secret to life is to go into every room every day – even if it's only for few minutes.

The sturdy independent upright citizen has become a neurotic dependent frightened wreck.

Theodore Dalrymple, *Not With a Bang But With a Whimper.*

#Sacrament

It was a frightening experience. Everything shook and shimmered, I didn't know what was going on. One of the people I was with said 'Oh it's just an earthquake – nothing to worry about'. Not having experienced an earthquake before I was worried. It's a strange experience to be sitting down and watch things that don't normally move swaying from side to side. Buildings, lamp posts, trees and cars. It lasted but a few minutes and then business as usual resumed.

Seemingly, the city I was in rests on a fault line. San Diego has its fair share of quakes. If you google 'earthquakes in San Diego' you'll find they have has many quakes as other countries have days of rain. Fault lines intrigue me. The fact that the earth has areas that are faulty and cause stress and distress as they move about shows that fragility is a part of everyday life.

The Sacrament of Reconciliation, or Confession, for me is a humbling experience. I simply have to recognise that I have faults. I have fault lines that run through me causing things to happen that I'd prefer not to happen. The sacrament is basically me handing all these matters over to God and asking for his grace as I live with my faults. The only good thing about them is that they throw me back on God's love.

The sacraments are all to do with the physical celebrations by which divine life penetrates our human histories.

James Alison, *Knowing Jesus.*

#Spirituality

If you visit Westerbork Concentration Camp in the Netherlands you will see the railway line torn from the ground and rising upwards as if to say 'Never Again!' I refer to this awful episode of history to uncover for you one remarkable human being. Her name is Etty Hillsum and she speaks into the storms of our age with relevant and precise words.

Her personal life is worth examining as it's not what you'd expect of a person with a deep faith in God. She was emotionally confused as she grew up in a rather dysfunctional family. In her early adult years she was sexually adventurous, was never involved with institutional religion, even that of her own Jewish faith, and she had a rather strange relationship with a therapist who hailed from the early days of Freud, Jung, and the emerging psychoanalytic tradition. Yet, Hillsum went beyond the self to what is beyond us all. She learned how 'to stop and listen to myself ... to sound my own depths' finding 'a basic tune, a steady undercurrent'.

For me there are two outstanding marks of her spirituality. Firstly, that she felt God needed her. Her faith gave her the conviction that it was her duty to mind God and keep him alive for all to see. For, as one commentator said of her, 'if people lose God they lose everything – their humanity, their integrity, their beauty as people, their life. They will disintegrate. It is as if God becomes vulnerable in those times and she [Hillsum] has

to look after him and cherish his heart'. She wrote, 'There must be someone to live through it all, and bear witness to the fact that God lived, even in these times. And why should I not be that witness'.

The second mark of her spirituality was her ability to see God in everything. Having journeyed into her own darkness and having allowed the love of God to transform her, she knew all else was possible. From the camp she wrote, 'I often walk with a spring in my step along the barbed wire. And then, time and again, it soars straight from my heart – I can't help it, that's just the way it is, like some elementary force – the feeling that life is glorious and magnificent, and that one day we shall be building a whole new world'.

Hillsum's story tells us that God's power is not limited. That in individual de-institutionalised human hearts his Spirit stirs. That, rather than trying to fill pews only, a Church has to show that belief in God enhances people's individual and communal journeys – in fact its more than this, the Church has to show that people disintegrate as human beings without God.

One way of thinking about the incarnation is to understand Jesus as someone who had deeply internalised the will of God.

Murray Milner Jr, *Understanding the Sacred*.

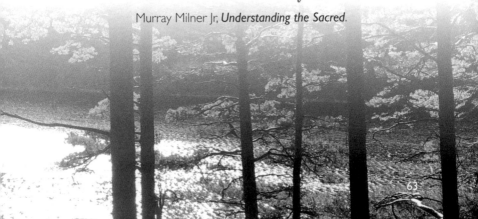

#Swimming

My mother wasted a lot of money on swimming lessons when I was young. Every week I went to the swimming pool, and I was terrified. I had a fear of putting my head under the water. I dreaded that moment when the instructor pushed us into the pool. I wasn't concerned about my swimming technique, I was just trying to keep my head above the water.

Thankfully somewhere along the way I overcame that irrational fear, and now I love swimming. I wouldn't consider myself a strong swimmer, and I don't like going out of my depth, but I love the ocean. I get energy from diving into waves, losing myself in the sea water and finding my way back to the air again. This is very much part and parcel of the summer for me!

Fear can hold you back from so much, even from things that are good for you. Submerging yourself in water involves letting go of fear, even overcoming irrational fear so that you can enjoy the refreshing and uplifting sensation. It is no wonder that the image of water is used so often in the spiritual journey. Even

Baptism, the first of the sacraments on a religious journey, is symbolised by water. This rich spiritual symbol speaks of dying to an old way of life and taking on a new refreshing way of being in the world.

But its more than one day. Belief in a loving God is a belief that you are carried by him through thick and thin. You can spend a lot of your days paddling in an immature spirituality and fail to immerse yourself in a presence that carries you and sustains you. Thomas Merton, after a lifetime of searching, expresses this sentiment beautifully. 'Life is a prolonged immersion in the rivers of tranquillity that flow from God and into the whole universe and draw all things back into God'.

Faith does not have to be faith in anything more than possibilities which one cannot see, meanings not yet revealed, values whose worth one will never have a chance to measure.

David Smail, *Taking Care: An Alternative to Therapy*.

#Sync

The Bible is a history of things being out of 'sync' and needing to be restored again. People bypass common human decency, the common good, or a dignified order to seek their own ends – and they end up 'out of sync'.

The economist and commentator Francis Fukuyama, in his book *Identity*, offers a viewpoint that could apply to today or to many of those difficult times mentioned in the Bible: 'Modern liberal societies are heirs to the moral confusion left by the disappearance of a shared religious horizon'.

There are numerous occasions in the Bible when things are so out of 'sync' that the word 'barrenness' is used. You may be familiar with those moments when the barrenness of society becomes a personal barrenness and is transposed on to people like Elizabeth, Sarah, Leah and Rebecca. However, barrenness is a precursor to something new. In scripture new worlds are created out of whatever chaos is at hand, barrenness is never the end. Even the barrenness of the Cross and Calvary brought with it something new.

Fukuyama also speaks of the economic distress he sees in the world today. He understands is it less as resource deprivation and more as a loss of identity; income and title are important parts of people's identities. This is why he said religion is so important and appealing. He says that in these moments of economic and social chaos the message is heard that 'You may be invisible to your fellow citizens, but you are not invisible to God'.

It took thirty years for television to achieve global reach — broadband made it in three years.

Gary Bouma, *Australian Soul.*

• • • • • • • • • • •

#Teaching

The era of television- and radio-generated panels of experts, who gave opinions on almost everything, was one in which you had no option but to agree or disagree with these experts – no one else had an opportunity or a chance to share their view or opinion.

The period of the expert, in the overall picture of things, was relatively short. Take for instance the world of traditional Irish music. For many years music was learned from people who travelled. They brought tunes and variations of tunes to places they visited and they shared them. While there they picked up new tunes and variations from those localities and brought them with them to the next place they visited. They weren't so much experts as fellow musicians. They sat in circles in homes sharing stories and tunes. However, over the last number of years experts have emerged. Radio and television raised experts on to platforms that were higher than any altar or pulpit in the land.

The new era of the internet has brought the expert tumbling down. Anyone can access anything at any time without recourse to the expert. Religion too has had its day when pulpits and their occupants became the most important tool in the communication of Christ's message. The Gospel can no longer be taught vertically from an impersonal source of power on down. If anything of value is to be communicated today, it has to be done horizontally from one person to another along social and egalitarian networks just like those of traditional musicians all those years ago.

It has been said that the existing processes of
education is that of the ruling classes, in
the sense that it comes from them
and engenders conformity with them,
depositing in the recipient alien words,
gestures, and values instead of stimulating
and evoking their own words.

Juan Luis Segundo SJ, *The Sacraments Today*.

#Technology

Tom Wheeler became the head of the Federal Communications Commission in Washington, D.C. in 2013. He has written some fascinating articles on the growth and impact of the new virtual age. It is easy to scratch your head and speculate about the impact of technology, including social media and the internet, on our lives. You can rejoice in the new-found advantages of technology and also fret about the security risks that all this new technology brings.

Wheeler uses an image to help people understand the challenges posed by new developments in technology. Trying to work out what the future holds is akin to working on a jigsaw puzzle without the assistance of the finished picture.

He is abundantly aware of the advantages and risks of new technological developments, so what guides him without the aid of the 'picture on the box'? At a conference of change creators who were discussing these issues, he said that there were two things that provide shelter for him in this new era of rapid technological development: history and faith.

History, he tells us, allows you to see how people dealt with similar challenges in their age. There are many examples from the printing press to the invention of the steam train to the telegram. You can look back with the luxury of the picture on the box but when these developments were evolving people struggled with the consequences, both known and unknown, for their future as individuals and as a society. For instance, in the *Contemporary Review,* published in London in 1895, Clifford Allbutt claimed that the 'whirl of the railways and the pelting on telegrams' would increase the rates of mental illness. The other item that provides shelter for him is faith as it reminds him at every juncture that there is something bigger than him!

We study the ancient scriptures for meaning in our modern lives because they tell the stories that provide insight into the universal human condition.

Tom Wheeler, *From Gutenburg to Google – The History of Our Future.*

#Touch

'See how she leans her cheek upon her hand', said Romeo, as he looked lovingly upon Juliet. She stood on the balcony out of his reach. 'O, that I were a glove upon that hand that I might touch that cheek.'

He could see her but that wasn't enough, he wanted and needed to touch her. Touch is the only sense of the five senses that depends largely on our will and desire, unless somebody touches us first. It is the one that is fuelled by emotion and desire and yes, even curiosity. It can be the action of love or hate, revenge or forgiveness. Those who hate recoil from touch; those who love get lost in embrace, they nearly become one.

You'd love to touch God. You might be able to see God alive in the world, you may be able to think endlessly of God and even hear God in silence. But just to touch him, feel him and acknowledge his presence would be so reassuring. In the Gospel the apostle Thomas felt this way. He wanted to touch the wounds of Jesus so he could believe, hearsay wasn't enough. Like Romeo he wanted more, maybe it wasn't greed, maybe it was just the sheer

hunger to believe and fill the emptiness of the previous week. He'd already been fooled at the cross when the one who promised so much disappeared, touching would put all that in the past.

People crave belonging, they crave communion. Most people want to belong to something that creates meaning, but it isn't easy. People can get oh so easily distracted by being busy. For Thomas he had to touch the Lord, for others to hear was enough. Each person has their own way of connecting with the divine. Like Romeo and Thomas, for you it may be touch. Whatever it is that helps your faith it might be worth bringing it to your mind for a moment. It can be a wonderful unshakable gift that you don't fully understand, a rational assent or just the way everything about the risen Jesus teases your senses. It could just be pure common sense! Whatever it is – name it, cherish it and grow with it.

A desire for communion has been part of you since you were born.

Henri J. Nouwen, *The Inner Voice of Love*.

. . . .

#Understanding

I first met Revd Billy Wynn in the Poolbeg Yacht and Boat Club. We were both dispatched there for the annual ecumenical blessing of the boats on the River Liffey. Having broken his ankle a few weeks prior to the event, he gave his blessing from the front passenger seat of the car while I stood on the quayside. He was many years older than I, but he was full of wit, wisdom and theology. We had a great conversation then, and we had many good conversations afterwards. He never spoke much about himself, but from others I discovered how fortunate I was to meet and enjoy the company of this 'big man'. Among other things he was the one who brought the Samaritans to Ireland. He wrote a letter to Revd Chad Varah of St Martin in the Fields in London who set up this highly valued, confidential telephone service, which is a great source of comfort to many who are lonely and distressed. When they read his letter of application they said, 'This was the type of man we wanted to start a branch of the Samaritans in Dublin'. The rest, as they say, is history.

One Trinity Sunday he proclaimed the Gospel in his parish church, and then he disappeared from the pulpit. For a moment people thought he was unwell as he'd gone behind the altar. He emerged in a few moments later in a flurry ... well it was an unusual flurry because here he was cycling a bike off the altar and up and down the aisle of the Church while giving his homily. Picture this strange, rather large, fully-robed Vicar, cycling up and down the aisle of his church giving his weekly sermon. The point he was making was that if you think too much about the bike and how it works, if you try to understand all the various pieces, well you'll be looking at the bits and thinking so much about them that you'll just fall off. Similarly, he said, the best way to understand the Trinity it to try not think about it too much, just accept it and get on with it.

Think for a moment – often you don't understand those you love but this doesn't stop you loving them or being loved by them. How many parents understand their children or even more so how many children understand their parents? If they loved each other in proportion to their understanding of one another there'd be very little love around. If I as a priest had to understand everything before I proceeded with it, I'd be doing considerably less funerals and even less weddings! For most things I just have to get on my bike and get on with it.

We can love completely what we cannot completely understand.

Norman McClean, *A River Runs Through it and Other Stories*.

#What'sTheStory

A number of years ago I spent time in the Australian Outback. Travelling through Alice Springs, seeing Ayers Rock and spending time in Kakadu and Litchfield National Parks was an experience that stands to me today. I must admit though, that as a tourist I was deeply unaware of the depth of spirituality and connectedness that surrounded me. You could not ignore the moods, the beauty, the changing colours of the landscape, however. I wanted to understand what the land was doing to my soul. In the end, the landscape proved to be a backdrop for an understanding of theology and God that I never could have imagined. I arrived a tourist, but I left a pilgrim!

In the years that followed I set about reading a lot about what is called 'aboriginal spirituality'. I discovered that there is a deep sense of being part of a greater story of the cosmos. Referring to their Christian faith one writer said, 'We live in his story, his sacred ritual is ours, he is our dreaming'.

To me the most powerful line is 'we live in his story'. It made me ask myself, 'What story do I live in?' I can claim to be a Christian yet live in a story that can, at times, be diametrically opposed to the Christian story.

Sometimes too you can be a prisoner of a story not your own. You can be wrapped up in a story of greed, vengeance or vanity. Your entire story can sometimes be captured by others who sum you up in a word or category, and you can then become that word: alcoholic, neurotic, victim, loser, and so on. You can find yourself living through the eyes of others, losing sight of your own value. Stories that tell you you're hopeless and will come to nothing are self-defeating; stories that tell you you're wonderful and special can leave you vulnerable when challenges come your way. To be fully alive you need to be in touch with the story that begins and ends in love, and for many of us that is the Christian story.

Some of the stories from your Dreamtime legends speak powerfully of the great mysteries of human life, its frailty, its need for help, its closeness to spiritual powers and the value of the human person.

Pope Saint John Paul, Alice Spings 1986.

· · · · · · · · · ·

#Wisdom

Someone once asked me 'Why is the wise person important?' After rolling out a few standard answers that didn't satisfy the questioner, I confessed I didn't know. The answer made me think. 'Precisely because they don't need to be'. I know many people whom I consider wise and part of their persona is humility. They are not trying to be smart or trying to be noticed – they are just wise people.

In previous centuries some universities had a chair of wisdom. They'd appoint someone to the post who had no academic career but they were known for their wise insights and a knowledge that was hewn from a well-lived life. Like the saints of old they were acclaimed by their peers.

The Old Testament has a portion of its books that are referred to as the 'Books of Wisdom'. Some faiths don't recognise these as part of the Bible, they consider them to be 'uninspired', others revel in their content. One commentator tells us that the wisdom literature was the possession of the people. It was their way of holding on to their God. When Solomon built his temple some people felt very put out, it was as if the king was saying that the God of the Temple was now more important than their God. Wisdom allowed the people hold on to their God as they understood him. Wisdom was not a gift you could buy or earn; wisdom was always a gift of God. Many sought after it but never achieved it. Others received it in bountiful measure.

A sense of one's relationship to the divine can help to reduce pride and egotism, but it can also make one arrogant or oblivious.

Murray Milner Jr, *Understanding the Sacred.*

#Words

The late Barney McKenna of the band, The Dubliners, was reputedly trying to convince a professor of linguistics that Irish was the best language in the world. He insisted that every word in the world has an Irish equivalent. The professor was being rather coy and suggested that there may be words for which there was no equivalent Irish word. Quite indignantly Barney asked, 'Like what?' The professor said, 'Like igloo – there are no igloos in Ireland so there is no need for a word for igloo in Irish!' Barney thought for a moment and said, 'Sure we have a word in Irish for igloo'. The professor, rather surprised, asked, 'And what is that word?' 'Teach* [Choc]Ice' replied Barney!

You can often use words without fully understanding them or thinking about them. For instance, the word 'resurrection'. Resurrection, for me, means two things. Firstly, it is an event that happened to Jesus in time and space, giving us all hope. Secondly, it has a profound message about the nature of God, that God is a generous God, that God gives life where nobody else can give life. God gives us hope where nobody else can give us hope.

So when you think of resurrection, let's not just think of that historical event and just the story of Jesus. Let us look beyond it to the generosity and goodness of God, and think of the things that we can thank God for each and every day in the beauty of this world and the great blessing of good friends.

* Irish for house

There were different ways of growing old, perhaps. Some withered first in body, others in mind, yet others in soul.

Elif Shafak, *Three Daughters of Eve.*

#You'llComeToNothing

I had many fine teachers. One particularly fine teacher, Mr Doogue, taught me in fourth class. He opened my heart and mind to the beauty of nature. He explained the breeds of birds and the varieties of fauna. I knew, within a few months, the difference between a fern and a fungus, the migratory patterns of Canadian Brent Geese, the habits of a badger and much, much more. Learning was effortless because we were led to the edge of wonder and drank it deeply. That year my heart got to school before I did, it ran up the long road ahead of me with sheer excitement and expectation.

There were other years when I was made to feel I was a failure and I'd come to nothing. When I journeyed up the same drive-way my heart was behind me and I had to drag it. In some ways being told you'd come to nothing was good preparation for life because when things went belly up you were half expecting it and so you weren't shocked. Today it's different. The pressure on people in school is more subtle. For a teacher to tell someone they are a failure or a waste of space would most likely be a punishable offence.

Today you are told you are marvellous, gifted and and unique, that the world is your oyster and nothing will get in the way of your giftedness. It's nearly as dishonest as being told you will fail. Those who receive constant reinforcement of their brilliance don't seem to be too happy when their brilliance isn't noticed by others or when things get difficult. And when things go belly-up, that can be very hard to accept!

Yes, you have great potential, but you will still have hard days. This doesn't mean that your life is worthless. I don't know how to get the balance right in education, but I think the finest teachers are those to whom your heart races. They don't play with words like failure or marvellous. They let you be and they move you on towards greater things. You know that in their presence your heart is respected, safe and renewed. If you are very lucky this place of learning may even be a classroom.

Remember it is your gifts that can destroy you.
Ancient Sufi Wisdom.

Index
of
Photographs
in order of appearance

Longford: Royal Canal, Newcastle Wood

Waterford : Mount Congreve Gardens

Dublin: Bull Island looking towards Howth

Meath: Laytown beach

Longford-Westmeath: Rainbow

Brazil gift

Longford: Corlea Bog Walk

Galway, Athenry: Disused Railway

Longford, Newtowncashel: work of Michael Casey, Bog Oak Studio

Lamp post in evening sky

Galway, Letterfrack: Diamond Hill Loop Walk

Dublin, Bull Wall: Regina Coeli

Limerick, Murroe: Glenstal Abbey

Clare, Spanish Point: Sunset

Bike in Slovakia

Kerry, Killarney: Cardiac Hill

Galway/Mayo: Killery Harbour

Kerry: Killarney National Park

Wicklow, Glendalough: Hiking with International and Erasmus Students

Dublin, Bull Island: Rippled sand looking towards Howth

Galway,: Statue on hill behind Kylemore Abbey

Longford: Corlea Bog

Dublin: South Wall, looking towards the city

Authors garden

Dublin: Poolbeg Lighthouse

Clare, Spanish Point: Sunset

Waterford: Congreve Gardens

Galway: Walled Garden at Kylemore Abbey